CREATIVE

PAPERCRAFTS

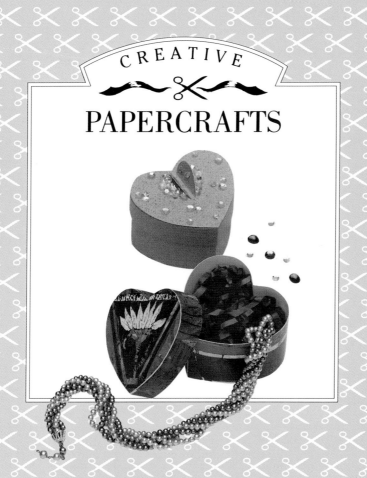

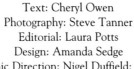

Text: Cheryl Owen
Photography: Steve Tanner
Editorial: Laura Potts
Design: Amanda Sedge
Photographic Direction: Nigel Duffield; Roger Hyde
Illustrations: Phil Gorton, Geoff Denney Associates; Richard Hawke
Production: Ruth Arthur; Sally Connolly;
Neil Randles, Jonathan Tickner
Director of Production: Gerald Hughes

CHARTWELL BOOKS
A division of Book Sales, Inc.
POST OFFICE BOX 7100
114 Northfield Avenue
Edison, N.J. 08818-7100

CLB 4326
© 1995 CLB Publishing,
Godalming, Surrey, U.K.
Printed and bound in Singapore
ISBN 0-7858-0283-5

CREATIVE

PAPERCRAFTS

CHARTWELL
BOOKS, INC.

INTRODUCTION

The papercraft projects featured in this book, including designs for party decorations, masks and gift boxes, require equipment most people have at their disposal. Indeed, it is the very accessibility of the raw materials and equipment that makes papercraft so popular. With paper readily to hand and without the need for expensive tools, there is no reason not to get started. Certainly, with care and attention a professional, lasting article can be created from the simplest of raw materials. However, before beginning there are a number of a number of points of technique that need to be considered. It is important, for example, to work with a sharp pencil and to use good scissors or a craft knife to ensure accuracy. Good quality paint and the correct type of glue will also ensure that the finished result is of the highest quality. For comfort and safety, work on a flat, clean surface taking care to keep sharp implements, glues and paints well out of the reach of children.

TECHNIQUES
Drawing
Use an HB pencil with a sharp point to draw with, as this will give a clear, fine line that is easy to follow. Accuracy is vital if the end product is to look professional, so it is important to use the correct drawing tools when you are working. Always use a ruler for straight lines and a set square when drawing squares or rectangles to ensure that the angles are correct. When drawing circles use a pair of compasses or if the circles are small, a circle stencil.

Painting

Painting paper to create the illusion of texture is a technique that has been used in one of the projects. Though many types of paint are suitable, using watercolour paints gives a soft, blended effect that is both pleasing and natural. For the best results, use a paintbrush that is suitable for the kind of paints that you are using.

Cutting

Though sharp, pointed scissors will be sufficient for most of the projects that have been included in this book, a craft knife will be easier to use and will give a neater cut. When using a craft knife it is important to replace the blade regularly as a blunt blade will tear the paper as it cuts. Always use a cutting mat or a board to cut on to, as this will not only protect the surface underneath but will also give a much tidier cut.

Sticking

Most of the projects in this book use PVA adhesive, spray glue or double-sided adhesive tape. PVA (polyvinyl acetate) dries to a clear, glossy finish and can be used as a varnish. Before using an adhesive, always read the manufacturer's instructions and test the glue on scrap paper before use. When gluing thin papers together ensure that the glue does not seep through the surface. Also, take care that the glue does not smudge the design on printed papers. If you are using a spray glue ensure that it is used in a well ventilated atmosphere with the surrounding area protected by newspaper. Double-sided adhesive tape has adhesive on both sides with a backing tape that can be removed when ready for application.

Specialist Craft Items

Cotton pulp and polystyrene balls, beads and sequins, along with any other extras that you may find that you need will be available from a craft suppliers and are relatively inexpensive to buy.

Making a Box Base

Cut out a box shape following the diagram provided (page 38/39). To make the box, score along the broken lines and then bend the card forwards along the scored lines. Apply double-sided adhesive tape to the back of the base tabs and to the right side of the end tab. Stick the base tab under the base. Then stick the end tab under the opposite end.

Making a Box Lid

Cut out a square pointed lid using the template provided (page 41). Then score the back along the broken lines. Bend forward along the scored lines. Apply double-sided adhesive tape to the tabs on the right side. Stick the end tab under the opposite side of the lid. Using the diagram provided (page 38/39), cut out the rim for the lid from white card. Starting at the tab end, stick the lower tabs to the rim, keeping the lower edges level. Stick the opposite end over the end tab.

Tissue Paper Honeycomb

Cut the motif from layers of tissue paper along the solid lines – the amount of layers needed is marked on each template. To cut through more than one layer accurately, staple the layers together first. Also, cut the motif along broken lines from card. Lift the tissue paper halves on one side except the bottom one. Dab paper glue on the bottom half close to the edge in the centre, then each side at 4 cm ($1^3/_4$) intervals. Press down the next half and dab glue close to the edge between the first positions. Continue to the top tissue layer, alternating positions. Glue the other half in the same way, then carefully stick the top two halves together. Glue the card sections together.

MILITARY MAN PARTY GLASS

This colourful glass trimming is easy to make and is a delightful table decoration for a children's party.

YOU WILL NEED:
Fabric napkins • Double sided tape • Silver paper • Black card
Green metallic card • Gold giftwrapping ribbons

INSTRUCTIONS

1. Begin by folding a brightly-coloured napkin into a strip 6.5 cm (2¹/₂ in) wide, roll it up loosely and place it in the top of a glass. Apply double-sided adhesive tape to the back of silver card and cut a shallow curve for a cap brim. Attach the straight edge to the glass rim. Cut out a moustache from black card.

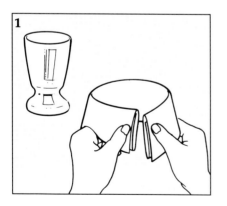

2. Apply a piece of double-sided adhesive tape to the reverse of the moustache. Attach a second piece of double-sided adhesive tape over the first and attach the moustache to the glass below the cap brim.

3. Cut a strip of green metallic card 3cm (1¹/₄ in) wide. Wrap around the base and trim to meet end to end. Cut the upper corners of the 'collar' ends in a curve.

4. Plait gold giftwrapping ribbons together and glue to the outer edges.

4

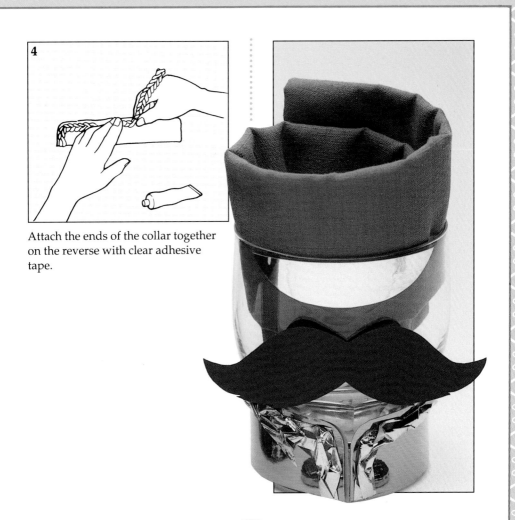

Attach the ends of the collar together on the reverse with clear adhesive tape.

TEDDY BEAR GARLAND

This delightful garland of paper teddy bears is relatively simple to make and is an ideal decoration for a children's party.

YOU WILL NEED:
Yellow sugar paper • Adhesive stars • Masking tape • 6 wires
Metallic card • Crepe paper

INSTRUCTIONS

1. Cut strips of yellow paper 10 cm (4 in) wide. Fold into concertina pleats 7 cm (2³/₄ in) deep. Draw a simple teddy on top. Cut through all the thicknesses, but do not cut along the folds.

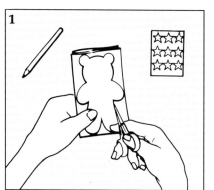

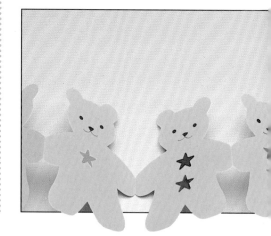

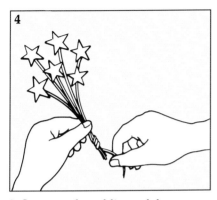

2. Open out the teddies and draw a face on each with a felt-tipped pen.

Attach self-adhesive stars to the bodies. Join the strips on the back with masking tape.

3. Cut 6 wires 15 cm (6 in) in length. Cut narrow strips of crepe paper, spread with glue and bind around the wires.

4. Cut out 6 stars from metallic card. Attach the stars to the ends of the wires and bunch together. Bind the end of one wire around the other stems.

5. Drape the bear garlands around the table with the bunches of stars between 2 paws.

Party Place Cards

Bring a touch of something special to your party with this unusual party place card.

YOU WILL NEED:
*Thick white card (to make the template) • Yellow card • Yellow tissue paper
Bright yellow marker pen*

INSTRUCTIONS

1. Using the template for a lemon slice (page 43), cut two circles out of pale yellow card for the front and back. Cut out the segments. Apply glue around the outer edge of one of the circles and

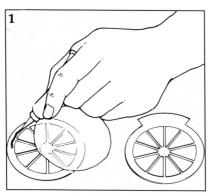

stick down a circle of bright yellow tissue paper. Glue the front and back circles together, with the tissue paper between them.

2. When the glue is dry colour the

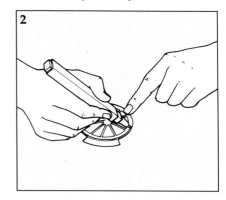

outer edges of the circle with a yellow marker pen to represent the rind.
3. Using a craft knife and steel rule, cut through one of the 'spokes' so that the lemon slice can fit on the side of a glass. Write the guest's name on the tag at the top. You could also make this place card as an orange slice using pale orange card and orange tissue.

PIRATE FAVOUR

*Bring a smile to the face of any small child with this
delightful party 'favour'. Filled with sweets and other
goodies, it will be sure to impress.*

YOU WILL NEED:
*Paper or thin card • Black card • Black wool • Spotted handkerchief
Brass curtain ring • PVA glue*

INSTRUCTIONS

1. Cut out a square of paper or thin card measuring 19 cm x 19 cm (7$^1/_2$ in x 7$^1/_2$ in). Fold the card into a cone shape, then carefully unfold it.

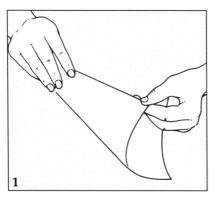

1

With a craft knife make a slit 2.5 cm (1 in) along each of the fold lines approximately 5 cm (2 in) from the top of the cone. Fold the card into a cone shape again and fix it together with double-sided tape.

2. Cut out a small semi-circle of plain card for the eye, colouring in the iris and the pupil. Cut out an eye patch from black card. Cut out a small cone shape for the nose. Attach them to the cone with PVA glue.

3. Cut out two semi-circles of card with a base 4 cm (1$^1/_2$ in) in length for the ears. Cut two slits, one on each curved edge of the two semi-circular ear pieces, approximately 1 cm ($^3/_8$ in) in

length. Make a small hole in one of the ear pieces. Insert the ears into the slits in the cone, ensuring that the ear piece with the hole in it is on the left.

4. Fold the flap of the cone over. Glue several lengths of black wool to the lid to represent hair. Tie a knot in a spotted handkerchief or remnant of material and glue it on top of the hair using PVA glue. Glue a brass curtain ring onto the left ear.

2

Seashell Favour

Decorate the cone-shaped 'favour' with a simple motif to make an eye-catching container.

YOU WILL NEED:

Patterned wrapping paper • Metallic paper • PVA glue • Water-based paint Double sided tape

INSTRUCTIONS

1. Using the seashell template (page 43) make a potato print. Choose a firm potato and slice it in half. Anchor the seashell shape to the potato with a pin. Holding the potato firmly, cut down around the shape using a sharp knife. Slice the flesh away right up to the edge of the design. The shape should stand proud.

2. Apply paint to the surface of the shape. Use water based paints mixed with PVA glue to give more body and make the paint more water resistant. Press the cut potato firmly onto the printing surface.

3. Print the shell motif onto a piece of patterned paper. Each paint application should last for two prints, fading slightly on the second.

4. Leave to dry, then glue to a piece of metallic paper, measuring 19 cm x 19 cm ($7^1/2$ in x $7^1/2$ in). When dry make a cone shape and fix it together with double-sided tape. Fold the flap to form a lid and fill with sweets.

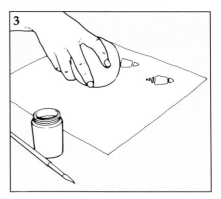

ROSE TRELLIS BOX

*This attractive box makes an unusual gift for Easter
or for Mother's Day.*

YOU WILL NEED:
*Green card • White card • White wooden bead • Dark green tissue paper
Pink or red tissue paper • Spray glue*

INSTRUCTIONS

1. Cut out a box from green card using
the diagram provided (page 38/39).
Cut out a square pointed lid using the
template provided (page 41) and
square pointed lid rim using the
diagram provided (page 38/39).

2. Apply double-sided adhesive tape to
the back of the white card and then cut
the card into long strips 6 mm (¹/₄ in)
wide. Stick the strips to the sides of the
box and lid, creating a diagonal criss-
cross pattern. Trim the strips so that

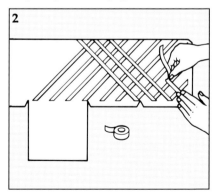

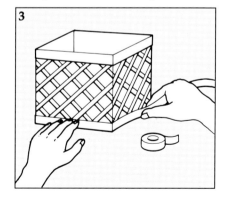

they are level with the base and edges of the lid.

3. Make the box and the square pointed lid following the instructions provided (page 10/11). Cut a strip of white card 41.5 x 1.2 cm ($16^3/_8$ x $^1/_2$ in) and attach to the lower edge of the box with double-sided adhesive tape.

4. Glue a white wooden bead to the point of the lid.

5. Stick 2 layers of dark green tissue paper together with spray glue. Cut a large number of tiny leaves from the paper and fold them in half.

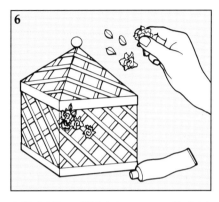

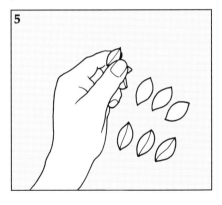

6. Cut 3.5-cm ($1^1/_2$-in) squares of bright pink tissue. Scrunch into balls and glue to the box and lid together with leaves as roses.

HEART-SHAPED GIFT BOXES

These charming heart-shaped boxes are ideal for presenting small pieces of jewellery and look pretty on a dressing table or bureau.

YOU WILL NEED:

Thick paper • Double-sided adhesive tape • Sequins • PVA glue

INSTRUCTIONS

1. Use thick paper for the boxes or apply giftwrap to thin card with spray glue. For the bases, cut out 2 hearts using the template provided (page 42). Also cut out 2 hearts for the lids, adding 1 mm (¹/₁₆ in) to the circumference in each case. For the beaded box lid, cut out a tiny heart along the solid lines using the template (page 42). Score along the broken line and lift each side upwards. Glue a piece of contrasting paper on the reverse of each half of the heart.

2. Refer to the diagram provided (page 40) to cut out 2 box sides and rims. Score along the broken lines on the wrong side and bend the tabs forwards at right angles. Apply double-sided adhesive tape to the tabs on the right side, then snip the lower and upper tabs to the scored lines at 7 mm (⁵/₁₆ in) intervals.

3. Matching the points of the hearts to the centre folds, attach the lower tabs of the box sides to the bases and the upper tabs of the rims to the undersides of the lids. Stick the end tabs under the opposite ends. Carefully glue sequins and small beads to the tiny heart of the beaded box, then at random to the lid.

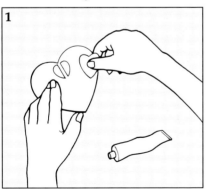

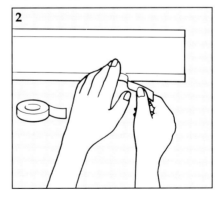

TISSUE PAPER CATERPILLAR

This tissue paper caterpillar, which is threaded through with wire and can be bent into the shape that you want, will be a lasting favourite with children.

YOU WILL NEED:

7-cm (2³/₄-in) polystyrene ball • 4 or 5 different colours of tissue paper PVA glue • Wire • 2 cotton pulp balls • 2 goggle eyes

INSTRUCTIONS

1. To make the head, tear tissue paper into small pieces. Apply to the polystyrene ball with PVA adhesive. Overlap the tissue edges to cover the ball completely.

2. Staple layers of tissue paper together so that several sections can be cut at a time. Then, using the template provided (page 43) cut about 135 sections.

3. Dab paper glue onto alternate scallops of the first section, then press the second section on top. Dab glue on the scallops of the second section, making sure that they are different to those glued on the first section. Press the next section on top. Continue gluing all the sections in this way.

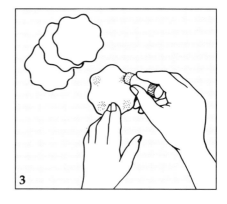

4. Make a hole through the centre of the tissue sections and thread a wire through it. Dab glue on one end and push it into the polystyrene head.

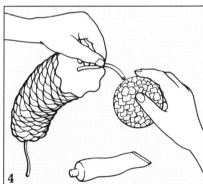

5. Cover 2 small cotton pulp balls with tissue, twist the ends and dab the twist with glue to secure. Cut off the twisted ends. Push the extending end of the wire into one ball.

6. Glue the first and last sections to the head and tail respectively close to the wire. Glue the remaining ball to the head as a nose.

7. To make the antennae, bend the ends of 2 lengths of wire into hooks. Cut narrow strips of crepe paper and spread with glue. Bind around the wires. Pierce holes in the head and insert the antennae ends. Glue on goggle eyes and a coloured paper smile.

BUMBLE BEE

*This delightful paper bumble bee will be one insect
that you will not be sorry to have in your home.*

YOU WILL NEED:
Yellow and black tissue paper • Yellow card • Frosted paper • Wire • Crepe paper

INSTRUCTIONS

1. Use the templates provided (page 44) to cut 46 bumble bee heads and middles from black tissue paper and 46 fronts and ends from yellow tissue paper. Cut 2 complete bees from yellow card.

2. Overlap each head and middle over the fronts and ends by 4 mm ($^5/_{32}$ in) and attach with paper glue. Make the bee following the tissue paper honeycomb instructions (page 11).

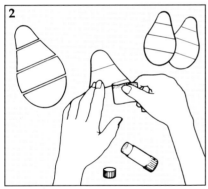

3. Using the template provided (page 44), make a pair of large wings from frosted paper. To do this apply double-sided adhesive tape to paper, remove the backing tape and place a wire along the centre of the strip, extending downwards. Starting at one edge, press a second layer of paper on top. Cut out the motif.

4. Bend the ends of 2 lengths of wire into loops for the antennae. Cut narrow strips of black crepe paper, spread them with glue and bind around the wire. Dab the extending wing and antennae wire with glue and insert into the sections on the bee. Hang the bee on a length of thread.

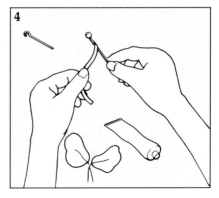

Rose-Covered Hanging Ball

Bring a touch of spring to your home with this delightful hanging ball.

YOU WILL NEED:

Bright yellow paper ribbon • Lemon yellow paper ribbon • Polystyrene ball
Patterned paper ribbon • Green paper ribbon

INSTRUCTIONS

1. Cut the bright yellow and lemon paper ribbon into strips of 25 x 2.8 cm (10 x 1¹⁄₈ in), cutting away the lower corners in a curve.

2. Starting at one end, begin to roll up the strip keeping the lower edges level and dabbing occasionally with glue to hold in place.

3. Make small pleats on the lower edge about 1.5 cm (⁵⁄₈ in) apart so the rose is not too tight. Cut across the lower edge so that the rose will stand upright on a flat surface.

4. Bind a 6-mm (¹⁄₄ -in) wide strip of bright yellow paper ribbon around a length of coiled patterned paper ribbon. Glue in place. Pierce a hole through the end of the coiled length of ribbon. Insert a long length of wire

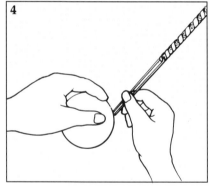

through the hole and bend the wire ends downwards. Push the wire ends through the centre of a dry foam ball and splay the emerging ends open under the ball.

5. Use the template provided (page 45)

to cut rose leaves from 2 shades of green paper ribbon. Gather up the lower straight edges and dab with glue to hold the gathers. Glue the roses and leaves to the ball to cover completely.

6. Cut a strip of patterned paper ribbon 34 x 8.5 cm (13³/₄ x 3³/₄ in) to make the bow. Fold in the ends to meet the middle point along the ribbon's length and overlap. Gather up the centre and bind tightly with a narrow strip of adhesive tape.

7. Bind the centre of the bow with a strip of patterned paper to make the 'knot', gluing the ends in place at the back of the bow. Glue the bow to the top of the rose ball.

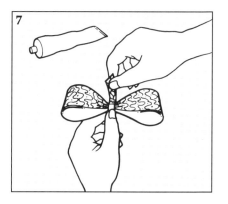

IVY WREATH

*Paper leaves, painted with watercolour paint, are used
to create this festive variegated ivy wreath.*

YOU WILL NEED:
Thick wire • Watercolour paper • Cream and green watercolour paint • Reel wire

INSTRUCTIONS

1. Bend thick wire into a circle 25 cm (10 in) in diameter. Overlap the ends and bind together using masking tape.
2. Using the ivy leaf templates provided (page 42) cut leaves from watercolour paper. Dampen the leaves, then paint them cream, adding pale green details and finally dark green areas. Fold along the 'veins'. Tape a length of wire to the back of the motif with the wire extending downwards from the leaf.
3. Bind wire with floral tape. Coil the wire around a pencil, then remove the pencil. Pull coil slightly open to form a tendril.
4. Bind the wire stems of the leaves around the base wire circle. Bind wire tendrils to the wreath. Bind the base ring with floral tape to neaten and secure the leaves and tendrils in place.

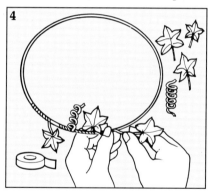

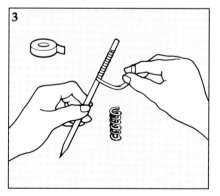

IVY-CLAD CHRISTMAS DECORATIONS

*These enchanting ivy-clad rings make unusual
decorations for the festive season.*

YOU WILL NEED
*Curtain rings • Willow rings • Cream paper • Watercolour paper • Watercolour paint
Florist's Tape • Masking Tape*

INSTRUCTIONS

1. Bind large curtain rings with narrow strips of cream paper, gluing the ends of the strips onto the backs of the rings.

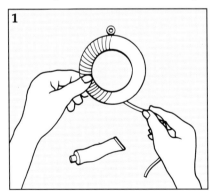

Use the templates (page 42) to cut small ivy leaves from watercolour paper for the rings.

2. To make the ring with dark green leaves, bind fine wire with green florist's tape and wrap around the ring. Dampen the leaves and paint with dark green watercolour paint. Fold the leaves along the veins. Glue the leaves directly onto the ring.

3. To make the ring with the bow, cut 5 leaves from watercolour paper. Dampen the leaves, then paint the them bright green. Then use a fine paintbrush to paint them deep red, making sure that fine green 'veins' are

left. Trim 2 leaves smaller than the others. Tie a bow of narrow paper ribbon and glue to the top of the ring. Glue the leaves to the ring.

TRAGEDY AND COMEDY WREATH

Decorate this paper wreath with masks made from gold paper to make a stunning wall decoration.

YOU WILL NEED:

Paper ribbon • Wadding • Gold spray paint • Gold card

INSTRUCTIONS

1. Cut 2 strips 85 x 11.5 cm (34 x 4⁵/₈ in) of paper ribbon and 2 strips of wadding 85 x 8.5 cm (34 x 3¹/₂ in).
2. Wrap paper strips around the wadding and staple the long edges together. Lightly spray with gold paint.
3. Twist the two strips together. Bend them into a circular shape, overlap the ends and tape together, making sure

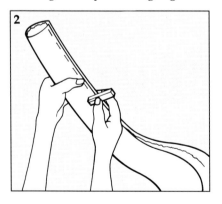

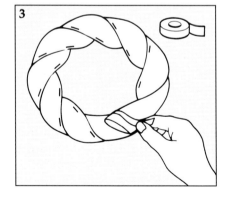

the joins are at the back of the wreath.
4. Cut a Comedy and a Tragedy mask
from gold card using the templates
provided (page 45). Pull the masks

between thumb and finger to curve.
Cut different sizes of stars from gold
paper. Glue masks and stars to the
wreath.

SQUARE BOX

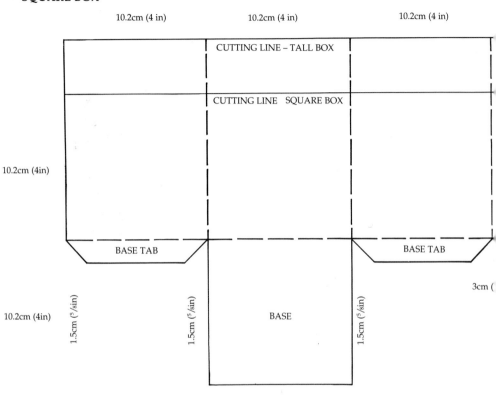

10.2cm (4 in) 10.2cm (4 in) 10.2cm (4 in)

CUTTING LINE – TALL BOX

CUTTING LINE   SQUARE BOX

10.2cm (4in)

BASE TAB

BASE TAB

3cm (

10.2cm (4in)

1.5cm (⁵⁄₈in)

1.5cm (⁵⁄₈in)

BASE

1.5cm (⁵⁄₈in)

SQUARE POINTED LID RIM

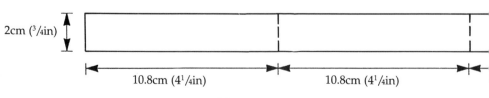

2cm (³⁄₄in)

10.8cm (4¹⁄₄in)   10.8cm (4¹⁄₄in)

10.2cm (4 in)

1.5cm (⁵⁄₈in)

14cm (5¹⁄₂in)

END TAB

BASE TAB

1.5cm (⁵⁄₈in)

1.5cm (⁵⁄₈in)

END TAB

cm (4¹⁄₄in)   10.8cm (4¹⁄₄in)   1.5cm (⁵⁄₈in)

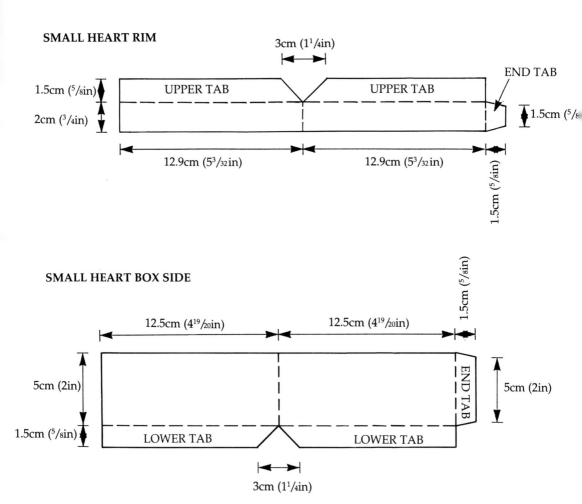

SMALL HEART RIM

3cm (1¼in)

END TAB

1.5cm (⅝in)

2cm (¾in)

UPPER TAB

UPPER TAB

1.5cm (⅝)

12.9cm (5³⁄₃₂in)

12.9cm (5³⁄₃₂in)

1.5cm (⅝in)

SMALL HEART BOX SIDE

1.5cm (⅝in)

12.5cm (4¹⁹⁄₂₀in)

12.5cm (4¹⁹⁄₂₀in)

1.5cm (⅝in)

5cm (2in)

END TAB

5cm (2in)

1.5cm (⅝in)

LOWER TAB

LOWER TAB

3cm (1¼in)

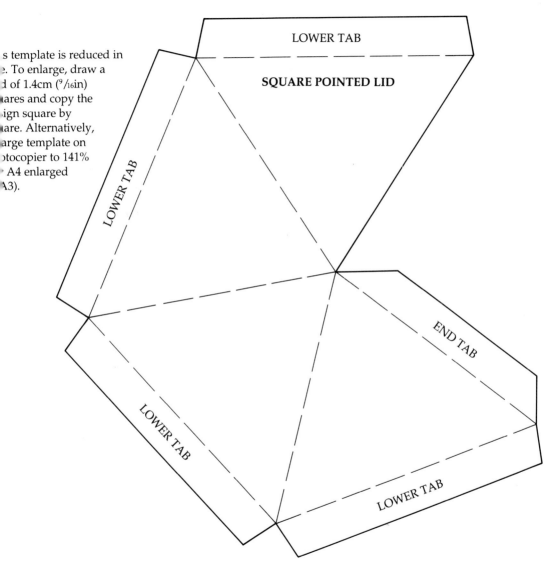

s template is reduced in
e. To enlarge, draw a
d of 1.4cm ($^9/_{16}$in)
ares and copy the
ign square by
are. Alternatively,
arge template on
otocopier to 141%
A4 enlarged
A3).

LOWER TAB

SQUARE POINTED LID

LOWER TAB

LOWER TAB

END TAB

LOWER TAB

LOWER TAB

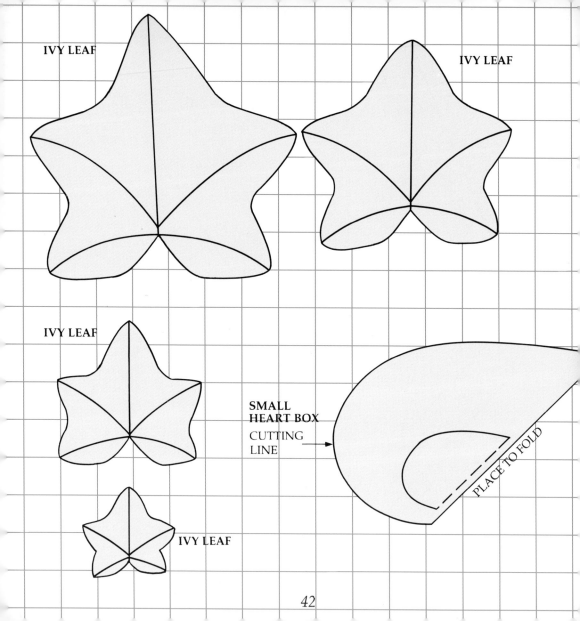

IVY LEAF

IVY LEAF

IVY LEAF

IVY LEAF

**SMALL
HEART BOX**

CUTTING
LINE →

PLACE TO FOLD

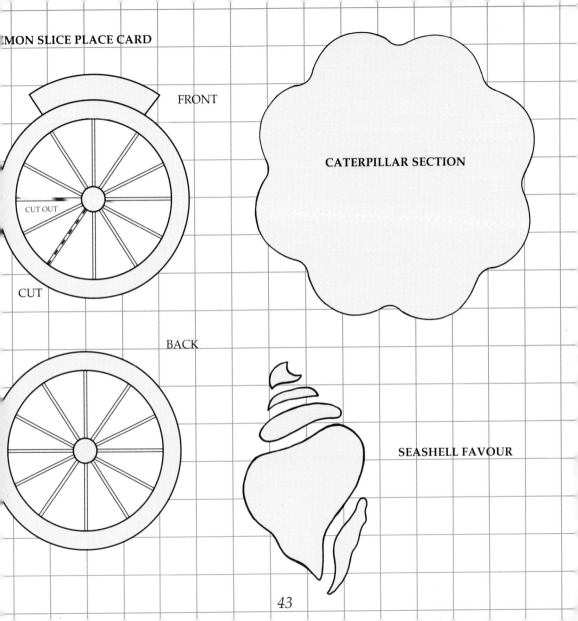

LEMON SLICE PLACE CARD

FRONT

CUT OUT

CUT

CATERPILLAR SECTION

BACK

SEASHELL FAVOUR

43

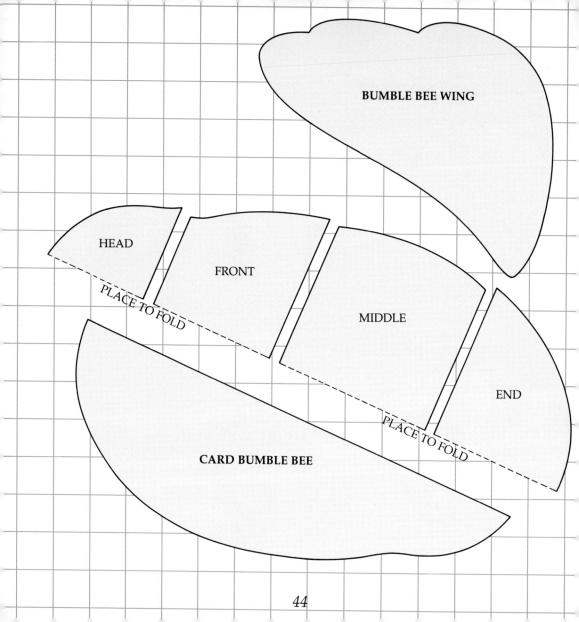

BUMBLE BEE WING

HEAD

FRONT

PLACE TO FOLD

MIDDLE

END

PLACE TO FOLD

CARD BUMBLE BEE

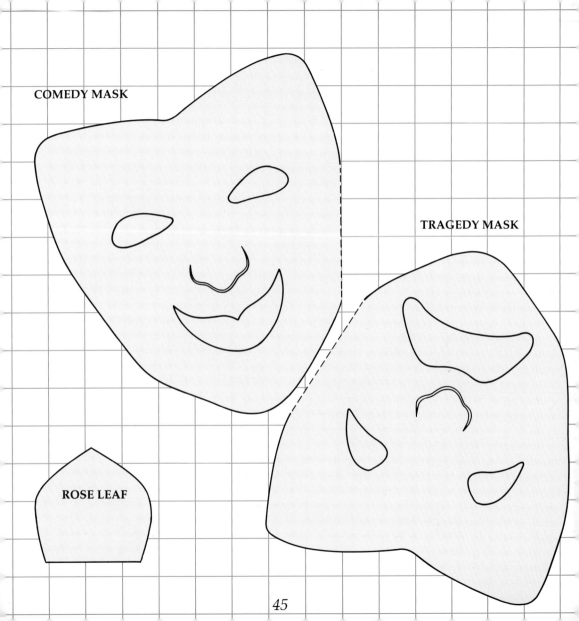

COMEDY MASK

TRAGEDY MASK

ROSE LEAF